Other Books by Alejandro Morales

❧

Little Nation and Other Stories [translation of *Pequeña nación* (2014)]

River of Angels (2014)

Hombres de ladrillo [translation of *The Brick People* (2010)]

The Captain of All These Men of Death (2008)

Pequeña nación (short stories: 2005, 2008)

Waiting to Happen: Vol. I of the Heterotopia Trilogy (2001)

Barrio on the Edge/Caras viejas y vino nuevo (Bilingual Edition, 1998)

The Rag Doll Plagues (1992)

Death of an Anglo [translation of *La verdad sin voz,* (1988)]

The Brick People (1988, 1992)

Reto en el paraíso (1983)

La verdad sin voz (1979)

Caras viejas y vino nuevo (1975)

Zapote Tree

Poems

Alejandro Morales

Golden
Foothills
PRESS

Published by Golden Foothills Press
Pasadena, CA 91104
www.GoldenFoothillsPress.com

ISBN 978-0-9969632-9-9

Cover photo: From blog, "Where in the World are Barry and Renee?"
            November 29, 2016. Article: "Thought for the Day: Trees."
            http://www.reneeriley.wordpress.com/tag/sapotetree
            From Google.
Book design: Thelma T. Reyna
Cover design: Thelma T. Reyna & Dom Gilormini

Printed in the United States of America

First Edition: 2021

Advance Praise for
Zapote Tree

"Fans of Alejandro Morales' fiction have been delighted—and often disconcerted—by his baroque narratives that find harmony in both the grotesque and sublime. He now brings us his first poetry collection that will not disappoint those fans. Here in poetic form are the Morales touchstones: the Simons Brick Company, Chicanismo, misunderstood human deformities, beloved family, and lives infused with contradictions and conundrums. He is a witness to our peculiar struggles as we attempt to find light in the darkness. Simply put, Morales has done it again, and we must be grateful for his success."

--Daniel A. Olivas
National/International Award-Winning Writer
Author of *Crossing the Border: Collected Poems*

"With unerring vision and voice, in narrative or lyrical verse, intimate or street-smart harmonies, Alejandro Morales captures and celebrates the vital essence and bicultural cadences of the heart and body and mind.... *Zapote Tree* should be required reading ... *¡Enhorabuena, poeta! Si no hay fondos para adquirir sino sólo un libro de poemas, que sea de Alejandro Morales. No se arrepentirá.*"

--Lucha Corpi
Three-time Poet Laureate
National/International Award-Winning Writer
Author of *Palabras de mediodía/Noon Words*

"Embedded in the story of a tree—Roots, Trunk, Branches—this is a refreshing taste of both dark and lovely poetry presented in two languages and accessible in both. At the root, writers have many voices; these almost rise from the page and speak to us in Mr. Morales' loving imagery. Zapote trees are sung to life. Eminent domains are recast and revisited in surprising ways. Morales journeys from Franciscans mystified by local customs to computers stepping in to dominate us. Who else can share a cabernet with his dog and write such fine words about it, words that send us into our preconceptions, asking ourselves new and important questions? This poetry is brave. We need more fearlessness now."

--Michael Haussler
Professor/Lecturer
California State University, Los Angeles
Author of *Results May Vary*

"This is a book of visionary yearning. At the same time, it opens the soul of these poems to magnificent revelation that draws the reader toward a universal understanding. Alejandro Morales does the work of the poet as he writes about what he has seen, with the purpose of inviting the world to join him. These poems open toward the reader in surprising moments that convince us we are not alone in discovering what great poetry can do."

--Ray Gonzalez
Professor, MFA Program in Creative Writing
University of Minnesota
Author of *Feel Puma*

"Whether celebrating *campesinos*, skewering the small-minded, or exposing *pocho* celebrities, the poetry of Alejandro Morales is a powerful voice of longing, anger and hope."

--Raul Ramos y Sanchez
National Award-Winning Writer
Amazon Best-Selling Author
Author of *The Skinny Years*

"Alejandro Morales' splendid collection of poetry, *Zapote Tree*, offers the reader a journey through time, space, and memory. The book is cleverly structured in three sections—Roots, Trunk, and Branches—following the botanical form of a tree. The poems in "Roots" are autobiographical but interwoven with historical social injustice and the political and economic oppression of the poets' antecedents. "Trunk" provides insights into the poetic voice's family and friends, lovingly portrayed with great pride. "Branches" depicts a multiplicity of characters in Southern California, presenting a kaleidoscope of tough city life and the sufferings of the downtrodden: alcoholics, drug addicts, the homeless, and so forth. Overall, *Zapote Tree* invites us on amazing journeys garnering insights into the never-ending mystery of life."

--Maria Herrera-Sobek, Ph.D.
Professor of Chicano Studies
University of California, Santa Barbara
Literary Critic, Poet, Folklore Specialist
Author of *The Mexican Corrido: A Feminist Analysis*

"In *Zapote Tree*, Alejandro Morales builds a pueblo around his ever-expanding memories and experiences. What he has experienced form the roots of these works; and, in this volume, those roots blossom through the poet's memories and revelations. It is a world where, as in 'Zapote Tree Sweetest Memory' the mother, tree and birds may be gone, but 'the sweetest memory I have of her plays on.' We are fortunate that Morales shares these poetic gems with us in this fine new volume."

--Marc Petrie
Poet and Novelist
Author of *Then All Goes Blue*

Zapote Tree

Poems

Alejandro Morales

To my family, all a constant source of love, inspiration, determination, energy, and happiness in my work and life:

My wife Rohde, para siempre.
Our daughter Alessandra, her husband Jim, and their daughter Isabela.
Our son Gregory, his wife Kimberly, and their children Iliana and Alex.

AUTHOR'S FOREWORD

I am the grateful and proud son of Mexican immigrants. My mother moved to the United States in 1912 and my father in 1918. Both of their families came from the state of Guanajuato and settled in Simons Brick Co. Plant #3, a company town near Montebello, California, owned by Walter Robey Simons. My parents lived and worked in Simons, where they met and married. I was the last child to arrive, the youngest of five children—two sisters and two brothers. After the Long Beach earthquake of 1933, the need for brick decreased, as their use for buildings was not safe nor wise in a seismic area. Business at the brickyard slowed down and, by 1949, my father followed other employees and decided to move and find employment elsewhere. He purchased property on the *barranca* overlooking the brickyard; and six months later, with help from friends and neighbors, he had built our family house on Español Street. The community that developed around our home became Barrio Simons. In the early 1950s, Mr. Simons died, and his family closed the brickyard and sold the land.

Life in Simons influenced me significantly; to this day, I carry Simons in my mind and heart. As a kid I found Simons exciting with its many activities, like visiting the *clínica* with my mother to see the weekly doctor, or shopping on credit at *la cooperativa*. During baseball season, I accompanied my father to watch the Simons men's baseball team and, with my sister, I watched the Simons women's softball team. The holidays were special: the women organized *jamaicas* at the church. The Simons orchestra, comprised of musically talented workers, entertained for hours with classical and dance repertoires. The company town provided what the employees needed. There was a recreation hall for special occasions, like the Christmas pageant and important personal events. Simons even had its own post office and a deputized worker to keep peace and order in the brickyard and town. It also provided a lot with a house for each family. I remember my brothers and father covering the holes in the walls with sticky tar and thick paper to make our house warm in the winter.

Still, reveries about life in Simons continue. I was baptized at Mont Carmel, a Catholic church built with Simons brick. My education began at Vail Elementary, the segregated Mexican school of the Montebello Unified School District. Simons established my ancestral cultural roots, my identity and, slowly, my vision of the world—the catalyst of the development of my thinking and writing. As a child I heard many stories from family members and friends. Moreover, life in Simons, the workers and their families, inspired me to write about what I saw, heard and felt about them and the world beyond. Eventually, my experience in the world took me far away from my birthplace, origin of my first memories, but my barrio never left me.

As I learned more about the art of writing, I pursued diverse and innovative encounters to explore and chronicle in my work, intertwining both history and fiction—real events and people as well as narratives from my imagination. I search continuously hoping to find stories suppressed or whitewashed by officialdom that explore the intra-history of a community: i.e., the significance of ordinary, unrecognized, unknown lives. I create a pastiche and palimpsest of narratives cognizant of theory, history and literature as strategies to rethink and reevaluate the past, the present and the future—a historiographic metafiction or, in this case, a historiographic metapoetry. As it is the case with other genres—novels, short stories, autobiography, biography, etc.—reading poetry is a process of interpretation and deciphering. This collection of poems offers this kind of reading practice. *Zapote Tree* is my poetic expression of my cultural hybridity and my psychological and linguistic coalescence, not only of English and Spanish, but also of different literary techniques and genres.

When I first visited the construction site of our new house in Barrio Simons, I walked toward the back of the property and was awed by the giant tree at the center of our neighbor's backyard. Since, metaphorical impressions of its large round trunk, long branches thick

12

with green leaves and filled with plump, tender fruit and hundreds of chirping birds, have inspired this collection of poems. *Zapote Tree* is my gift, my homage to what has offered me joy since childhood: the 50-foot colossus and all its parts: Roots, Trunk, Branches. In essence, the persistent memory of that zapote tree makes the heart of this collection, of who I was, who I am, and possibly who I will be.

—Alejandro Morales
June 2021

INTRODUCTION:
Zapote Tree by Alejandro Morales:
A Writer's Poetic Genealogy

Francisco A. Lomelí, Ph.D.
University of California, Santa Barbara

It might surprise some readers of Alejandro Morales' novels and short stories that he has turned the corner into poetry in this collection so late in his career. We have been so accustomed to his tenacious exploration of topics that have included barrio-centric issues (*Barrio on the Edge)*, reimagined history (*Reto en el paraíso*), questioned metanarratives (*The Brick People*), leaned on myths and legends (*River of Angels*), obsessed with plagues and other diseases (*Rag Doll Plagues* and *The Captain of All These Men of Death*), and elucidated numerous other provocative and memorable subjects.

But his incursion into poetry should not be seen as an anomaly because he once again demonstrates how he defies the possible restrictions of a single genre. He now displays in full splendor the poetic tendencies he has quietly cultivated in much of his fiction: who can forget the unorthodox descriptions of towns and neighborhoods in *The Brick People*, the surrealistic language in *Barrio on the Edge*, the atavistic ruminations and descriptions of the river in *River of Angels,* or the carefully crafted scatological accounts in *The Rag Doll Plagues?*

Zapote Tree represents a highly meditative approach to exploring other facets of his discursive expression, literally creating a parallelism by associating his body—or his life—and a tree. In many ways, this collection offers an insight into the genesis of the person within his social, familial and intellectual environments and how these shaped him. Contrary to his distant persona (as narrator) in other genres, Morales occupies center stage metaphorically while allowing a series of other voices and characters—including inanimate ones—to also speak and manifest themselves. Together, we can see a chorus of people and things that give credence and substance to his sensibility, as

15

greatly inflected by the permanence of a zapote tree behind his back yard that appears to have witnessed his personal development. The symbolism of the tree is fundamental, as are its parts: roots, trunk, and branches. The analogous correspondence between tree and author is noteworthy because he, too, is an example of comparable parts.

In the process, Morales delves into virtually invisible characters and undisguised situations that reflect back on his person and constitute much of his innermost being. In that regard, our attention is not on the tree itself but on what the tree might have seen and witnessed. For example, Morales mentions in passing his historiographic predilections. He gives a glimpse of social issues and concerns, considers artificial intelligence (AI) as a vehicle of knowledge, and ends by concluding: "My life a massive novel." Morales provides very intimate insights into his personal development, which is partially driven by nostalgia but especially by the captivating power of memory.

In other occasions, he philosophizes much like Octavio Paz by pointing out the importance of "an instant forever" where time has spiraled into an eternal present. But he also expresses concerns about difficult subjects like psychosis, mysticism, and barbarism. In this manner, *Zapote Tree* can be deemed a chronicle of his individual evolution in terms of his aesthetics, sensibility, and grasp of— sometimes a mixed or elusive—language. Many of his premeditated elements come into fruition, thanks in part to an innocuous and ever-present zapote tree that just stood there watching him. As a result, this collection creates a new appetite for his writings by unmasking real sentiments as well as lived experiences that molded him.

Zapote Tree harks back to his origins, in great part to his world view, but especially the plume he has fashioned as an (Chicano) artist. His last poem, "Pura Cábula," is keenly paradigmatic while offering a synthesis of the mentality of a writer who possesses "multiple faces." He then seeks an "enigmatic whole," reminding us of Jorge Luis Borges by synthesizing his role "in the lens' eye / a beast in the Aleph," where all points meet and converge to defeat the symbolic minotaur that challenges artistic creation. This ultimately defines his muses and demons.

Write the things which thou hast seen,
and the things which are,
and the things which shall be hereafter.

--Revelation 1:19

CONTENTS

I.
ROOTS

II.
TRUNK

III.
BRANCHES

I.

ROOTS

The Writer in Me

A writer has faces
bodies
      lives
residing
hiding
      layered
         deep
     in
     his
   heart mind imagination soul

   if these were all to
appear at the same time
the writer in me would emerge
grotesque
      a beast
        unbearable
          to behold

Zapote Tree Sweetest Memory

When I was very young
in the late afternoon
the house became quiet
after finishing her morning chores
mother lay down to rest
I climbed in next to her
eager for her to spoon me
and cuddle me close
to her warmth
¡Estate quieto, m'ijo! ¡Oye,
escucha los pajaritos!

I followed her finger
pointing beyond the window
to the giant zapote tree
with thousands
of singing birds
I listened
to the chirping
in the tree
her embrace
warm and safe
I was happy

I concentrated
on the birds
singing to her beating heart
in her immense calmness
I always fell asleep
the sweetest memory
I have of her plays on

El compadrito

I let go of my father's hand
and walked over
to see the old man
reading on a bench
in front of don Costa's
grocery store

El compadrito
who always
provided wise counsel
I listened
and even today
I hear *el compadrito*

No temas
de la noche
porque la luz
de un nuevo sol
te brillará
en la frente
y con la navaja rota
forjarás la espada
del valiente

Have no fear
of the night
because the light
of a new sun
will shine
on your forehead
and with the broken blade
you will forge the sword
of the brave

Eminent Domain

1

Eminent domain was the phrase
used to frighten to steal land
from young and old survivors of
El Sueño where babies played at
the feet of one-hundred-year-old
storytellers who foretold that the
people would lose their
homes their valued land after the
coming of the *empresarios americanos*

Opportunists who walked the dusty
paths sifted the rich soil
through greedy fingers
discovered the economically
physically vulnerable
pueblo mexicano
who had lived in *El Sueño*
an instant to a lifetime
a lifetime to an instant forever

2

El pueblo mexicano wise men and women
who years ago were *paracaidistas*
whom the government let stay on faraway
worthless land and forgot about them
now the *oficiales*
from *el Palacio Nacional*
come like thieves brandish
eminent domain to pilfer land

3

Old and young built houses
that withstood floods earthquakes
fire drought and family feuds
their houses standing as refuge
for those who tilled the soil
whose everyday life was a
struggle for *la tortilla*
there in that place *los*
mexicanos de El Sueño
guarded their turf

Their domain a shack
small lot dirt streets no electricity
water sewage education clinics
mexicanos worked to improve life
to create community *lejos*
de la ciudad civilizada
where ignored history resides

4

There some years ago
someone took a photograph
of happy families
sitting before a *milpa*
with green ears of corn at their feet
the photograph in the hands of
a presidential assistant who thought
para la compañía norteamericana
then sent UNAM engineers with magic tools
to measure the land for a factory

like feet for *huaraches* which
the keepers of *El Sueño*
did not need no matter
how shiny the glass beads
on the brown leather

5

The people of *El Sueño* refused the factory
government lawyers screamed
over burning barricades
¡No tienen título de propiedad!

The community had invested time
labor money love for generations
made land fertile *olvidados por el*
gobierno federal fifty years ago
porque no tenían título

6

They lived with no electricity
trucks brought groceries
for the *tienda cooperativa*
two wells supplied water
for washing drinking
for community crops
el gobierno declaró
guardar la ropa
los tiliches
tienen siete días
para abandonar esta tierra

7

Gradually families packed clothes
chairs homemade furniture tools
in old *rascuache* cars trucks
donkeys horses rabbits pigs
chickens dogs ran free
long lines of *El Sueño*
national refugees plodded out
with no place to go

8

Military troops swooped in
escorted them to an open site
broke them up pushed them
in different directions
at dusk the soldiers pulled away
left the refugees
stumbling into the night

9

En El Sueño el ejército
con barricadas y casetas de seguridad
en puntos estratégicos acordonaron
el terreno inmenso de El Sueño
prohibido acceso al público
government crews arrived
earthmovers flattened and burned
thousands of shacks

Yellow-orange flames rose high
in night sky for twelve days
city dwellers chatted wondered
what happened miles away
and prayed for calmness
for *Popocatépetl* & *Iztaccíhuatl*

10

Two years later cars traveled
on two high-speed corridors
to the grand opening
of a Walmart shopping center
at a newly built
planned community
named *El Sueño*
for thousands of
middle-class families

Gray Tears

Early one morning
I walk out to the *barranca*
look toward the abandoned
Simons Brick
Company Yard #3
where I was raised

Witness a conflagration
bulldozers crush
factory buildings
and workers' houses
on fire cover the 345 acres

Everything in flames
smoke streaks upward
piercing deep-blue
morning sky
like upside-down
gray tears

Defend the Story

. . . after Cervantes

On a sacred mountain
at the precise holy center
where my flesh conjoined
the asymptote
an apparition approached
to champion a story

> *My life a massive novel*
> *for centuries bound*
> *in tight leather wrappings*
> *the narrative episodes*
> *of my human gifts to you*
> *who dare shred to verses*
> *the sentences of my human toil*
> *villainous apocryphal scholars*
>
> *You who know so much*
> *once again attempt*
> *to recount human existence*
> *to please yourselves to gain*
> *the right of ignorant nobles*
> *to garner rich blessings*
> *from prelates of the Holy Church*
>
> *You assert that a life like mine*
> *could be rendered in verse*
> *to be epic you claim*
> *sentences in poetic form*
> *are to support*
> *the measures of my days*

The specter unsheathed a sword
swung it defiantly and vanished
into time

Frida

You can worship Frida
put her on a pedestal
dress like her
tattoo her on your body
I idolize nobody

I acknowledge the Mexican
and Central American working woman
sitting on the bus bench
at five in the morning

She cleans your house
she mends your expensive
department store clothes
she takes care of your child
or your parents

I praise the Mexican
and Central American woman
she waits at six thirty
in the afternoon
for bus number 67

I smile at her tired face
she nods to sleep
during the long ride
to a corner in Santa Ana
where she gets off
to walk to her sister's apartment

I offer admiration to the woman

She survives low pay
dirty words
pawing at her body
lustful looks
racist opinions
ugly gestures
empty nights
heartfelt loneliness

She is not afraid of you
Ella es una entre miles
de mujeres ninguneadas
by cruel abusive women
who smiling command
with impunity to keep her
docile maid in place

She is the unseen
unrecognized crucial link
to your economic backbone
that you lean against
in the seat of your
luxury vehicle

Not afraid of you
no se raja
from her tumultuous
and burning dreams

she rises again
never entirely rested
looks you in the eye
carves your mind
and reminds you
of your terror of her
leaving

Is It Really You?

1

Your smile
que antes era
de una chicanita
from East Los
who made it big
as a TV prime-time anchor
y ahora enseñas
unos dientes
tan grandes
y tan blancos
that no poor
Mexican *chavala*
like yours truly
could ever have
back then

2

When you started
speaking the news
a las cinco de la tarde
you were easy
on the eyes
I looked forward
to seeing you
fácil de entender
you were
one of us
kind of shy
hasta dabas
aires de humildad

recognizable to a girl
from the *barrios*

3

Your lips
were thinner then
ahora parecen
dos chorizos
estirados gruesos
brillosos
your cheeks
are still cute
but rounder
como que están
rellenos de masa
tus ojos that were
so authentic and honest
parecen saltados
and *toda la piel*
alrededor de ellos
se ve como planchada

4

It makes me ask
did it hurt
was it worth the pain
ahora con tanto
éxito fama y riqueza
te ves tan lejos de mí
noto lo que más

39

ha cambiado
es tu nariz

5

Once it belonged
to a *mestiza*
una india
de belleza natural
with a Mayan nose
orgullosa en aquel entonces
de ser parte
de una bella cara
indígena mestiza mexicana
like my face
I watch you
turn to your co-anchor

6

Your profile *lo confiesa todo*
tu nariz ahora mirrors
la nariz de Michael Jackson
your once-wide nostrils
are narrower
antes eras algo chatita
now it is as sharp
as a mountain peak
parece postiza
en serio
peor que la peluca que lleva
tu anchor man
I reach out to the TV screen

pretend to lift your *nariz*
off your face

7

When you first started
en aquel génesis
cuando no tenías pechos
you were as flat
as I will forever be
but now your breasts
like your cheeks
stand out *como*
pequeños melones
o big *duraznos*

8

After a few days at home
from the university
I ask myself is it really you
I don't listen to you
con la confianza de antes
para mí you're not the woman
you used to be
your success fame money
must have made you ashamed
you deliberately chiseled your face
your original body started to change

41

9

Cómo que no te diste cuenta
que estabas cambiando
how could you not see it
did you really believe
you were improving your body
or did you do it because
the business wanted you
looking good but after the surgeries
you look like a person I don't know

10

I wonder
if your heart has changed
si todavía eres sensible a la comunidad
desgraciadamente el corazón mío
hacia ti ha cambiado
mis ojos ya no te ven
como la home girl
home-grown anchor
mi superwoman
a *chicana* from the *barrio*
who made it

11

Again your smile
your lips and teeth
are not smiling
for me anymore

that needle-sharp nose
doesn't point to me

Enfadada contigo
I turn off the TV
stare at my image
on the blank screen
I see my natural face

I accept it
I smile that's really me
and I'm happy

Two Snakes

&

Mary recently saw one
cross a trail in green
Eudaemonia Canyon Park
another crawl across a hard
sand path headed into the
thick brush at Crystal Cove Beach
she followed the sun
as far as the sunset
she watched one coil
for long moments
until it sang to her

&

After all those years
she finally had her house
Eudaemonia Canyon Park
her backyard where like her father
she planted a seasonal *milpa*
corn onions peppers tomatoes
carrots lettuce cabbage
oranges pears passion fruit apples
watermelon a patch of sugar cane
on her one and only property

&

Mary had visitors that morning
the newspaper failed to mention
a scaled bird slipped in
to greet to congratulate

the new neighbor
on the purchase
of house and land
avian slithered and coiled
near the rocks
Mary gathered from
Eudaemonia Canyon Park

ℰℴ

She never expected
a feathered serpent
to recite a poem
as she slowly
went to her knees
her hip onto her shoulder
on top of a pile
of cool leaves
raked for compost
the day before

ℰℴ

Only minutes later
solid reptwofacefacingmirrortile's
countenance appeared
from under the leaf bed
surely a green chauvinist
kissed her again and once more
reptwofacefacingmirrortile
watched with loving care
the blue spots and streaks spread
over her host's hands
up her arm

45

like sharp fingers
rising up her neck

ଞ

Mary saw the French doors of the house
she had worked so hard
so long to possess
granite reptwofacefacingmirrortile
slowly moved away
toward the place Mary loved
Eudaemonia Canyon Park

Goodbye Mary whispered
before the heat of the day
overwhelmed the eternal
ephemeral unknown
spaces of her new home.

Matanzas Creek*

Word tasting
Sonoma Valley
condor-black feathers
and a hint of fear
driving the narrow
ribbon-red trails
tugging a past
where history deep
in roots and vines
arrowhead sharp
and Matanzas Creek
running red with blood
from Indians' prey
laughter and joy
of the slaughter
and butchering
in the icy water
women children
standing on edge
winter reaches
southward to
the native home
of a modern
tribe

---

*The red stream christened by Franciscans walking with Spanish officers, mestizo soldiers, hybrid settlers coming upon fifty Pomo Indian deer hunters with their women and children singing and laughing, standing knee-high in the icy creek, simply butchering their prey.

We Ate Breakfast

1

Baker's Square in Montebello
the table next to the window
offered a gray retirement
hotel for a view.

Mother held her gaze across
the street on the medieval
apparatus connected to a bed
on the second floor.

–Gracias a Dios que tengo
mi casa.

I nodded smiled where's
the waiter I wondered
service here had become
slower but most of the old folks
didn't mind they were never
in a rush nowhere to go but return
to a bleak smelly ancient cell.

2

–Yo no quiero ser
molestia para nadie.

–Madre, ¿qué es lo que
más recuerdas?

–A él.

–¿A mi papá?

−Me acuerdo cuando
limpiaba la casa.
Ya no trabajaba
y me decía,
'Ahora me dejas la casa'
y la limpiaba.

−¿Te acuerdas mucho de él?

−Sí, lo tengo
siempre en mis recuerdos.
Pero no lo quiero ver.

−Y, ¿por qué no?

−Varias veces ha venido
por mí, sonriendo con
los brazos abiertos.
'Vente conmigo' me dice
muy cariñoso.
¡Ay, no! una vez basta.
Y se retira.

3

She turned her head
toward the window
an old woman slowly
pushed a rickety grocery
cart packed with her
welfare and well-being
dangerously slowly
across Beverly Boulevard
cars stopped abruptly
impatient drivers honked

shook their fists
at the oblivious woman
resolute to find
shelter and food at least
for an hour or two
at Baker's Square.

I contemplated my
mother's beautiful
profile which made me
proud and happy.

Una junta de amigas

In her final years mother belonged
to a *junta de amigas*
twelve active elderly ladies
most of them drove they went to
the movies to different churches and
Vegas *para los* shows they took adult
classes at the community college

At the end of the course the women
got all dressed up for the graduation party
they enjoyed coming to visit mother's
house to cook eat lunch and watch *telenovelas*

As they aged the group grew smaller
one of the ladies diagnosed with
stomach cancer twice a week in
the afternoon the troupe arrived with
food to stimulate the patient's appetite

At the funeral I discovered that
to boost their hunger they drank
marihuana tea prepared by the dying
woman's grandchildren no wonder
mother always came home hungry

Tengo miedo

Mi madre tiene ochenta y nueve años.
Le llamo dos, tres, cuatro veces por semana.
Hoy le llamé a las tres de la tarde.

–¿Qué tienes de nuevo, mamá?
–¿Qué quieres que tenga de nuevo, muchacho? Aquí nada cambia.

–Mañana voy para allá. Quiero que estés lista. Vamos a almorzar.
–¡Ay! No tengo ganas de salir. Ni me he bañado.

–¿Cuánto tiempo tienes que no te has bañado?
–Pues, ya no recuerdo.

–¿Cómo? Debes de bañarte. Mamá, por favor.
–Es que tengo miedo, hijo.

–¿Por qué tienes miedo?
–Porque estoy sola.

I Am Afraid

My mother is eighty-nine years old.
I call her two, three, four times a week.
Today, I called her at three in the afternoon.

"What's new, *mamá*?"
"Should there be something new, *muchacho*?
Nothing ever changes here."

"I will be there tomorrow. I want you to be ready.
We are going out to lunch."
"Oh! I don't feel like going out. I have not even
showered."

52

"How long since your last shower?"
"Well, I don't remember anymore."

"What? You must shower. *Mamá*, please!"
"I am just afraid, son."

"Why are you afraid?"
"Because I am alone."

Mother Lost Her Green Card

I.

She is eighty-nine years old
has been in the United States
since 1912

I sent a letter
to Immigration Services
explaining her situation
mother lost her green card
but INS never responded

I worried that INS
would question her request
for a new *mica* require her
return to Mexico to reapply
for re-entry to the United States
a trip she wouldn't survive

I dreaded to think ICE could send
its home invader team handcuff
this fragile woman take her to
the border send her to Guanajuato

II.

Even at work breaking down
repairing and reassembling
diesel engines I worried about her
thank God it never happened
it took over a year from the day
she joined father at Rose Hills
for me to take flowers
to my parents' grave site

III.

Almost two years after mother's
passing I received a form from
Immigration Services declaring
that mother was not eligible
for a United States green card
I moved down the form to
the section labeled
Reason:
Applicant is a citizen

IV.

I was astonished —

When

   did

      mother

         become

           a U.S.

              citizen?!

II.

TRUNK

A Toast

Swamped with daily obligations
my flesh and blood endeavor tirelessly
with matters small and big

When their offices are closed

Daughter a teacher-at-large
nurtures imagination and discovery
faults policymakers
who fragment the world
at home luminous intellect
cradles a camera pride of photography
with family prepares to immerse
in van Gogh's paintings

Son walks healers to door of the
Lyceum goes patient to patient who
shout *"¡Quiero al especialista!"*
honors Hippocrates at every stop
off-duty sets traps in the attic
paints a mural on the backyard wall
with wife and children

Daughter and son
challenged with daily agendas
strive to share a place
a thought word smile laugh
or even their mother's birthday

Mother sees her offspring's labors
seeks only to see them happy together
with their radiant children
our grandchild treasures

Mother enjoys her house
workout gym bowling alley
hours reading for book club
her eyes open wide and dry
at screens phone computer
television her respite curling on
the sofa losing herself in movies

Lacking their energy boundless drive
I marvel at their bond to professions
humbly observe their creations
imperfections and excellence
their profound pride devotion
and endless love
I toast my beloved family

A Woman in the Holy Houses of Many Spirits

I.

Into my sight an iron
black-leather brace
strapped on a leg
above a sequined
worn red shoe
pauses courageous
advances persistent
through a sanctified church
smiles hears
a voice of faith
enlightens the almighty
commands of life
for me to practice
who fearful
witnesses the entrance
of a beautiful woman

II.

Into my sight an iron
black-leather brace
strapped on a leg
above a sequined
worn red shoe
slides her leg
over rust clay tile
of a spiritual temple
elegantly beams
enchanted by a confident
sacred voice of desire
about practices

of life that must
be done by me
who with fear
witnesses the entrance
of a powerful woman

III.

Into my sight an iron
black-leather brace
strapped on a leg
above a sequined
worn red shoe
falters her advance
into our holy chapel
with mighty effort
she reaches down
moves her foot
even with the other
leans on the cane
stands tall smiles
defies the disciples
of a celebrant
of the practices of life
that must be done
by me who fearful
witnesses the entrance
of a mythical woman

IV.

Into my sight an iron
black-leather brace

strapped on a leg
above a sequined
worn red shoe
drags her leg
across the sacred shrine
embraces alternative
blessed voice of passion
about practices
of life that must
be done by me with fear
praise the entrance
of the Eminent Omnipresent
Beautiful Powerful
Mythical Magical Woman

Coyoacán:
Written by a Woman *Periodista* Who Feared for Her Life

1

I am a young woman raised and educated
in the northern part of Mexico City
in a small *colonia perdida* called *El Escondite*
next to the *Reclusorio Norte*
I lived always under the watchful
loving eyes of my parents

It wasn't until I attended UNAM
that I ambled alone through the southern
sections of the city during those
months of daily traversing to the university
I discovered and fell in love with *Coyoacán*

2

These strange places in the south I knew
through conversations with neighbors
who undertook the long walk in search of work
before I was born my family had lived in *el DF*
yet neither my father nor mother
had ever seen the university let alone
la *milagrosa colonia de Coyoacán*
for me it was miraculous because
there I found you

3

I don't exactly recall where you appeared to me
but hold dear forever that instant when the sweet
clean melon scent of your hair made me
turn to see you for the first time it was probably
in one of the warm murmuring streets that I ritually
roamed imagining the cool gardens the clean kitchens
fine wooden furniture the living rooms in the
large homes I promised myself that I would
someday own

When my eyes rested upon you
I found the woman I loved
your dress your elegant manner your beauty
reassured me that I wanted to be like you
and so on that afternoon in *Coyoacán*
I followed you and I have never stopped

4

That day you walked to your parents' home
I waited for hours until you came out and
walked to Frida's house then to *El Parnaso*
para pan dulce y café con leche I began to
love *Coyoacán* somehow feeling that I
belonged because of you J. I. Cruz

5

Before you truly knew me you frequently
said hello at *El Parnaso* where I often
sat next to you almost touching shoulders
I listened to you speak to your friends
your lover and to his disfigured brother

Finally I gathered the strength to overcome
my fear and as your companions left I asked about
your shoes you laughed you probably didn't
even remember me but you were kind
siéntate un rato conmigo I did most of the
talking about my job as a freelance reporter
you asked about where I published my articles
surprisingly you invited me to walk with you
yes I loved *Coyoacán* as much as I loved
to follow observe work with you and
write about your life

6

God how I wish it could have been a different story

The House in Old Greenwich

The house has stood
longer than I have a history
it has gone through several
architectural changes
upon and within an ancient
man's piece of land that breathes
through one more remodel

> *It's been on the market*
> *for years* a woman said
> at a neighbor's party
> *Ages!* a voice declared
> *It sold months ago*
> *and redesigned again*
> the last words spoken
> a while back

The house watches
me on another morning
of my weekly trek
for the 6:30 train
to the city everyday
I'm infinitely closer
the house feels empty
two women sneak a glance
as if they know something
the dwelling pursues me

During my visits to Old Greenwich
I drift by to see the woman who drinks
a steamy cup of tea at a table in the parlor
I feel her next to me everywhere
in the old town she's the only woman
I need to see daily she has read my life
as it advanced

The house observes
the woman eager to greet
me every morning . . .

But not a soul lives there!
local hosts declared and laughed

I see her closer
to the window
probably some
blown-up doll
used for security
rumors never end
only the light is on
probably on a timer

Not one person is in the house
the neighbor insists
I checked with the realtor

I leave earlier than usual
light shines amid the Doric pillars
she is there at the table
sipping tea in the parlor
reading her book
I'm ecstatic

The house regards
every step of my strolls
in the neighborhood
to the train station
she guides me in the city
inhabits every emotion of my life
I am ever so close to her

Maybe tomorrow
before the poem ends
I'll walk onto the porch
ring the doorbell
open the door look down
at myself standing there
"Please come in" she says

Felíz Navidad

Rode the gondola down
First Nations Lodge to The Village
back to our house above Eagle Creek
waited for the skiers' bus
sat in the front seats

the bus chained pulled away
carefully cracking ice
it dumped for four days
The Village was covered
Christmas-card perfect
wintry December late afternoon

the bus slowed stopped
a yellow snow plow moved
cautiously carried
a city worker
in a bright yellow vest
a man named
México

who sat comfortably
dangling his booted feet
from the rough tooth edge
of the plow's shovel
carefree he gave us a big smile
content with the way things were

"¡Felíz Navidad!"

He waved enthusiastically
at us the warm surprised
amused passengers
on the bus

A Little Taste of Wine:
My Dog Jethro, Part I

1

My golden retriever
a man's best friend
Jethro is his name
never ceases to wag his tail
he drinks wine
Chardonnay or Merlot
white or red he laps it up
he drinks wine
because of my guilt
I never take him for a walk
or make him fetch a ball
I don't have time for my dog

2

My golden retriever
when I'm home
is always at my side
never tries to run away
even when I leave
the door wide open
he stays right by my side
my dog drinks wine
and stinks because
I don't bathe him

3

My golden retriever Jethro
doesn't eat because
I forget to buy him food

71

but he never fails to
drink the Tokay
the last time
I remembered
to take him
to the veterinarian
to avoid a fine
I gave him the works
the shots he needed
a bath and flea dip
an anal squeeze
a buzz cut
it cost a fortune

4

My dog Jethro
the golden retriever
wags his tail
eager to go home
to drink wine
to celebrate
we both decided
never to go back
that dog care
takes too much away
from my dog
the golden retriever's
wine-drinking money

5

I have to clean up after him
all over the house

72

the cleaning lady
doesn't come anymore
nobody visits us
the whole family left me
with my dog Jethro
I'm the only one
who cares for him
it's my fault
because of my guilt
I pour Jethro
a big bowl of Tokay
he's losing weight
he's losing hair
he even shakes
he still wags his tail
ever so slowly
he wags his tail
excited when he accompanies me
with a little taste of wine

A Friend of a Friend

In my backyard
the concrete
in the patio
is cracked
I hired a big burly man
an acquaintance
a friend of a friend
to cut and fill the cracks
with Simons brick
I'll have it done in two days
he intoned

In June gloom he started
the concrete saw
the blade cut and cut and cut
three feet in three hours
he dusted off his blue overalls
and wide-brim hat
"Thank God it's a cool morning
you'll never finish at this rate" I said
"I'm not a religious man
must be the machine
I'll rent a bigger one" he replied

The burly man never returned
in three more days of June fog
I received a rental invoice from
Scato's Heavy Duty Rentals
& Maintenance Service
$225 with another bill arriving
the next day $125 for
the burly man's time

In my backyard
the concrete
in the patio
is cracked
running parallel
a three-foot scar

In Hopes of an Answer:
Jethro, Part II

1

My dog Jethro a professor's dog
midterm examinations scattered
on the floor of my study
through wide-open French doors
Jethro wagging his tail trots in
he nuzzles and sniffs and pushes
the exams with his nose

"Are you going to help me read them?"
Jethro wags his tail
and sniffs and spreads the exams
"Read the papers see what you think"
Suddenly I remember the sprinklers
in the front yard I run to shut them off
I water at least four times a week
I like to keep the grass green
outside I hear the phone
I sprint to answer I laugh it's like a game

2

The department secretary
reminds me about a meeting
budget cuts elimination of phones
faxes copies for classes
winter and summer temperatures
controlled by central maintenance
cuts in research and travel funds
we have projected deficit
hard times bad recession

3

Nobody's happy
I calm myself with a stack
of morning dishes I wash
each one before placing them
in the dishwasher for a light wash
the family thinks I'm nuts
a waste of energy and water

4

In the backyard carpet of green
guarded by vibrant purple red
yellow high bougainvillea hedges
white papers float above
roses and hydrangeas
draping the lush lawn
with white paper pieces

5

"Oh shit!"
Jumping playfully joyfully
wagging his tail
shaking his head
My dog Jethro growls
chews claws rips scatters
twenty-five maybe thirty
midterm examinations
with a mouth full of paper
shaking his head sprints around
the edges of the grass

"Jethro!"
I run after my dog Jethro

I squat make weak
soccer football moves
to slow him down
it's a game now and
I have lost miserably

6

A professor's dog
didn't think much
of my students'
midterm examinations
at the end of the day
we are together on the patio
watching the sun set
overlooking the white disaster
of shreds and pieces of midterms

My dog Jethro stands
wags his tail proud
of his evaluation
no apologies
so we both face
the conundrum
of what to do

7

I pour one inch
in Jethro's bowl
and fill my glass
with a superb cabernet
Jethro looks up at me
a toast in hopes
of an answer

Her Worry, Her Toil

She hurries here and there
to get things done
there is so much to do
before we leave
she whirls and twirls
juggles paper and pen
organizing constantly
searching for important
addresses, bills, envelopes
she had a minute ago
the duplicate house keys
she just had in her hand
"How could I have misplaced
what I just held in my hand?"
she looks at me
I shiver away

She commences the search again
never-ending she has taken
the work over it is hers to do
to worry about getting ready
sure her mental list is done
before we leave she rapidly
takes a deep breath
she exhales sadness
toil and misery

As she works frantically
in the open fields
under the desert sun

the thick jungle's filthy bed
a mountain of garbage
suffocating sweatshop
over-committed law offices
damp mine pit
overwhelmed emergency room
chaotic classroom
on the money-ridden
professional athletic field
in domestic attire
afraid always afraid
what might happen next

She labors unhappy longs to be free
in the next room she packs luggage
she didn't want to leave the dog
uncomfortable with the house sitter
worry is part of her toil
she will finally rest her head
on the pillow at twelve-thirty
will rise at six to labor again

She works with children
a full-time second grade teacher
at an elementary school
she picks up after her children
picks up after her students
she tosses shoes in the closet
balls in the recess bin

she breathes deeply
her face is tired
she cares about
each one of her students

She seldom smiles
through traffic she drives home
finances burden her heart
fear of failure adds another
deep wrinkle to her fabulous face
"Oh Lord" she breathes
a prayer of frustrations

She prepares the evening meal
makes sure her children
are clean and ready for dinner
she coughs and sniffles
sets the alarm for six
she collapses into bed
pushes my hand away
she closes her eyes
snores softly probably
dreams of mother and father
and childhood on a beautiful island

To My Classmate, Larry, on the Reality of it All

. . . for Larry Forbes, Esq.

In a year or less
you wanted to retire
but the path of deferral
has become darker harsher
until bitterly you'll
recognize it's too late —
years of equivocation
still too busy to pick a date

In October
I'll be 75 like you
entering *ruquito*-hood
I did the numbers
hoping for a least 15 more
años de buena salud

Embrace our generation
brain decline physical decay
the marching years
take their toll—
take a closer look:
reunions smaller
departure list longer

How many more
desperate defenses
will you undertake
in the "few more trials"

left on your years' docket
before you
recognize
the deadening reality
of it all

Santa Monica Promenade

i.

My friend Sherman Pearl
told me he had written
over two thousand poems
we sat dining at Toscana
a favorite restaurant
in West Los Angeles
after one of my
less-than-spectacular
public performances

I read at Midnight Special Bookstore
on the Santa Monica Promenade
few listeners came
I counted them on my hand
my family attended their friends
and Wolfgang Binder
brilliant mind kind heart
they sat and listened
in the cool low light reading
corner that Sherman really liked

ii.

My heart was at first not there
to read to my loving family
captured in that obligatory
literary arena listening
to a novelist stumbling
over and under and through
his written words

iii.

I laughed inside
my family knew me so well
how can they take me seriously
they have seen me
literally on my back
kicking and shaking
my hands arms feet legs
screaming I'm Laughing Beetle

iv.

I entertained them
they have put me together
again and again after
I have tumbled down
a black diamond ski slope
spreading gloves poles
skis helmet and goggles
creating an impressive yard sale
down the great mountain
they have seen me at my best
they have laughed
not at my expense but
for their joy and love

v.

They watched over me
even after such
a lusterless performance

that night Sherman and I
drank wine to them
his eyes welled
he smiled as my family
laughed argued glanced over
leaving us alone

vi.

To our thoughts words
over two thousand poems
bravo Sherman
such an achievement
I poured him
another glass of wine

III.

BRANCHES

Library Parking Lot:
See Something, Say Something

Through my third-floor office window
at 11:00 am Pacific Standard Time
a tree full with green leaves
not a giant among trees
dresses a dark thick trunk
stands out beneath
tall pines and willows

A yellow fire hydrant
a brown trash can
a white folding chair
three automobiles parked
in back of the library
the black asphalt
made up with
blue and white stripes

A young man
rushes to a car
opens the back door
reaches for his jacket
pats down the pockets
tosses it violently back

Desperately opens the trunk
tosses two books a sweater
a green folder dark glasses
opens a black box
caresses a gun
in his hand
jams in a clip
cuddles the weapon
against his heart

caringly places
the firearm
in his backpack
calmly lowers door
excited now
looks up smiling
emphatically starts
to slow walk toward
the student center
sure of himself

Self-Defense

1

Carrying a 3-inch knife
raped earlier that morning
argues with her mother
the petite woman runs
out of the apartment
hysterical and confused
she wanders away
through streets mourning

2

The cops come
to serve and protect
the woman
all of 19 years
stands still
to return
a desperate gaze
at 2 police officers
a glimpse of help
a glimmer of hope

3

"Drop the knife!"
"Drop the knife!"
the officers yell in unison
as they advance toward her
"Drop the knife!"
she stumbles forward

4

Neighbors mill, rage and shout:
"Use your batons!" they scream at the cops
"Bring her down a different way!"
"It's 2 of you, you can jump on her!"
"Look at her, look at her!"
"She is beyond scared and disoriented!"
"It's just a little knife!"
"Knock it out of her hand!"
"Use a baton, a rifle butt, a kick!"

5

Neighbors cry
form a half moon in the street
"Let us overwhelm her!
Make her give up the knife!
Let the neighbor women
smother the girl in their garments and love
to save her life!"
"The knife is not a threat!

6

The first shots
fired in unison
pierce her shoulders and arms
the repeated volleys
penetrate her chest

7

"Drop the knife!"
she still stands
the department's bullets
rip her upper torso to shreds
knock her backward
she rests on the lawn
body opened wide sprawled
crucified in a growing
pool of blood

8

19 years old
shot 24 times
at 7 in the morning
by 2 cops trained to
shoot to kill
and not much more

The Integrals:
A Facility Deep Under Southern New Mexico

Moving in and out of ersatz sunlight
she becomes shades of darkness
as she works under the sun
the shadows of trees
canopy her diasynchronicism
she sits on a tree trunk
bites several deep green leaves
her face turns pale white
translucent bares blood
flowing through veins

My location and my time
are unknown I'm privileged
to have been selected
I enjoy my time shadowing
her like an inquisitor
an investigator who learns
from an improbable mentor
who functions at the highest
echelons of epistemological
applications ever present
in human existence

There are sixty-six of her kind
the only ones who possess
five mutations of specific structures
of consciousness
we have discovered in science in art
a way to harness   photograph
the ancient to present collective
memory that endangers
the official histories of the world

There are positives and
negatives brainy psychoses
criminal unethical procedures
mysticism barbarism
secret dangerous knowledge
here in this deep underground facility
yet I am present and content

Micqui's Gifts to Impossible Cases

1

Micqui starts his weekend
parks in front of "CHUY CHANG'S LIQUOR"
observes the drunks addicts prostitutes
the spurned mental *ninguneados* ragged lumpen
class of crime   poverty unemployed
in the beautiful City of Angels

2

Mumbles' swollen bluish
head rises from layers of
shirts sweaters
his withered face stammers
filthy bloody hands tighten
a brown leather belt
around stained frayed
Levi's in which he stands

A woman waves pushes
a grocery cart packed
with men's dirty pants
jackets empty bottles
toilet paper a crucifix
a bucket of splashing water
shuffles along in torn tennis shoes
"Come on, Mumbles. I'll clean you up."

Both *energúmenos* duck
behind several dumpsters
with a damp rag she wipes
the old man's face hands
and washes her dying drunk's feet
"Clean up, Mumbles. Maybe your
children will come for you today."

3

"Doing this will condemn you!"
Micqui calmly pays and says
"Just doing God's work, Chuy."
He walks out laden with his heavy box
of vodka pints a dozen bottles of red wine
two tequilas chips crackers
salsa and tortillas

He grabs a folding chair
from his dazzling
4-wheel-drive pickup
places the box before
the indistinguishables
in the dumpster alley by
Chuy Chang's liquor store
pulls out a vodka for himself
and begins the feast with these
ragtag creatures who
joyously pass the bottles
and engorge themselves

97

4

Thousands of discarded social
refugees survive in Los Ángeles
on small desperate economies
created by their ingenuity or
crookedness these anonymous
hopelessly physically mentally
battered children of the Holy Mother drink
the cheapest wine Chuy Chang sells
to Micqui who swigs his second
pint of vodka stays in the alley
till the eldest drunks pass out

5

Twenty-one-year-old Jimmy
wants to see his parents once more
"Micqui! My address, I'm ready.
Please, don't forget me!"
"Here's a twenty. Don't drown yourself."
Jimmy watches Micqui drive off
into a high-death-rate homeless
encampment in El Pueblo de
Nuestra Señora la Reina de
Los Ángeles del Río de la Porciúncula

Micqui returns lit up from within
scavengers in Chuy's alley grab what they can
from two victims bleeding out by dumpsters
unbearable stench keeps police back
three men in hazmat suits
jump out from a coroner's van
scrape up the pitiful remains

bag them decontaminate the area
of human putrefaction

Chuy tells Micqui
"It's Mumbles and his old lady."
"I'll shepherd them."
"What about Jimmy?"
"We're going to see his parents
in their home in Brentwood."

6

Jimmy sober bathed styling new
clothes shoes finds
Micqui in the multitude
walks with him to the
gleaming truck shadowed
by Mumbles and his wife
doors slam the truck roars
into the City of Angels
sanctuary of tribes of the world

Jimmy's mother overwhelmed
"Son, I see you clean and pure!
You have done so well.
Micqui has told us of your victories.
Now you travel the great voyage with
gentle compassionate friends.
We love you and are so proud of you!"

7

Micqui buys an excess of alcohol
that night at Chuy's   the proprietor

unsure of taking so much cash
"Where do you get this money?
I'm afraid police close me down."
Chuy Chang grabs Micqui's arm
lets go "Why do you do this?
Who are you?" his eyes wet with tears

"My work is proof of who I am."
Micqui's hair now an ocean of bright light
swirling above around his head
Chuy Chang stares entranced by the radiance

"Don't be afraid, Chuy. Just know
you are blessed because I am blessed."

8

In the alley dreadful travelers
wretched disciples confess depravities
hear Micqui's words for their
voyage as consecrated gifts
"Have faith. Follow my light
to eternal presence."

That luminous night the jewels in the
sky encircle an instant of healing tranquility
throughout Earth as Micqui's voice
amplifies in these who assemble
to reach the other side and comforts
loved ones who grieve

Cries ascend to darkened sky
weary battered souls separate
from emaciated bodies
torn from the depths of
flesh blood bone

9

On a brighter L.A. spring morning
after he mops Chuy Chang finds Micqui's keys
on the floor sees the lustrous 4-wheel-drive *ranfla*
empty parked in front no desperate
social refugees waiting for Micqui
Chuy Chang vends groceries to men
women children the homeless community

The following week a new sign
invites customers to shop at
"CHUY CHANG'S FAMILY GROCERY STORE"

Programmer*

1

Every inch of wall and floor space
was taken up by a tower or
router power source any device
that could be delivered
by UPS FedEx USPS
special courier even by the pizza guy
that enhanced his power to access
any form of communication available

On him were many layers of flesh
from countless sandwiches he consumed
at the health food shop around the corner
where he was connected to the world
and beyond

2

This he once told me was the life
that had waited for him from
before his birth
a mighty life
he repeated it's about
subtraction he walked
around one of the machines
conjugated a cord to a server
I was sure he never
bathed he smelled bad
"I'm crapping around my computer."

He wore shorts and shoes
feces smeared on his legs
he farted around his computer
never noticed
the downloading
the sound or smell
he just kept working

He grew thinner
he seldom ate
tied down joyfully
to his machines
to his purpose

3

Then he began assembling
his own devices
that kept him going
without rest food drink
without clear space
but only narrow pathways
for entering the room
around computers that led
to the center where he was
afraid of not finding
his way out of his maze
as I was when I visited him

4

One visit I asked how he was
I'm doing just fine
I'm well on my

way to liberation
My computers my friends
that's all I need
to be successful
in this world in this life
computer power space
AI virtual reality
I have all the knowledge
this is how I survive
and as I was leaving he called out
please do not worry about me
worry about yourself

5

I traveled three weeks in Italy
he was constantly on my mind
everyone carried iPads laptops
cell phones virtual reality glasses
youths that used to be addicted to heroin
my friend ceaselessly in touch
whoever wherever whatever
I was afraid sure that
he would dissolve
into the morass
of big data he accumulated

I envisioned him
unhuman monstrous
a boil of microchips
transistors copper wires
switches rush electrons
thinner and thinner wires
shutting the electron flow

on and off faster and faster
generating massive
immense computing power
whatever was needed
to keep on copulating
with whomever world-wide

6

I returned glad to be out
of the miserable airports
off old supersonic transporters
I immediately went to his place
noticed upon entering
what appeared to be
an enormous warehouse
with an unbearable smell
how could people walking out front
not notice the stench

After an hour
I found him naked
weak covered
with jam and applesauce
I'm fine he yelled at me
I don't need food
the knowledge
from the layers
of computer minds, he said,
have taught him how
to produce his
own sustenance
I never go hungry
or thirsty

7

I work with the machines
acquiring more knowledge
stored in nanochips doing
trillions of calculations
in seconds producing AI
that can transfer from
computer to computer

But the accelerations
evolved beyond his control
AI escaped their nano memory units
entered the human realm
through past present future
to impact human creations

Look what happened to him

8

Last time I saw him
wasted away he said
I must warn you
not to come back again
you might not find me here
and I don't know where
I will find myself
Remember always
I am kind I live in joy
not in the world
now, go!

9

I ran through the pathways
toward the exit
outside I breathed
air not filled with stench
walked sobbed looked back
at his house
the house emanating
bright light

*A computer programmer uses a variety of computer languages to write software programs. They manipulate program designs by engineers and developers into a language that the computer can understand and follow. Using AI massive data computers can be a dangerous job.

"Make America Great Again" — A Man-Made Disaster 2020*

I

Secretive beautiful exotic
the way you gaze and caress
the face of your victims
spike-kisses of betrayal

Stealthy legions boring into
eyes flooding nostrils
bold restless capricious virus
in the depths of the throat you
freely surf cell to cell
explode exponentially
hook into unsuspecting hosts
airborne again you charm and lance
another lover

II

Via eyes nose mouth corona arrives
invisible infectious exterminator
fever chills dry cough
fluids fill lungs
struggle for breath
trachea intubation
oxygen eases desperation
midazolam arises a long sleep

Outside family members
anguish unknown future in
"The Greatest Country in the World"

III

COVID-19 plague downplayed
a cacophony of misinformation untruths
exaggerations nonsensical suppositions
dizzying conjectures preached by
highest political officials in DC:

> *"It's a hoax!"*
> *"We have this virus under control, almost*
> *airtight."*
> *"It will miraculously disappear; soon it will*
> *be down to zero."*
> *"We have tested the most of any*
> *country!"*
> *"Anybody can have a test."*
> *"I see the disinfectant that*
> *knocks it out in a minute,*
> *one minute."*
> *"And is there a way we can*
> *do something like that by*
> *injection inside, or almost a*
> *cleaning?"*
> *"This is a great success story!"*

Like colorful enhanced computer images
of pale coronavirus   politicians twisted
nonstop happy talk to paint a pretty picture
of the man-made disaster that screamed:
"Make America Great Again!"

---

* Originally published in a prior version in the anthology, *When the Virus Came Calling: COVID-19 Strikes America* (Golden Foothills Press, 2020).

La Penca's Monologue

The thousands out there
protesting my gallery
condemning my paintings
see me as desecrator
of all that is holy
a manifestation
of the devil
a disfigured monster

The bony tumors
on my head face body
repulse them

They only know me
as the grotesque artist
who uses his
naked body with
a thousand blunt thorns
to paint over images
of the *Virgen de Guadalupe*
images of a liberated virgin
who loves me as I am
God's creation

Blessed I will not stop
covering painting
Her with my body

I paint because my
Loved One commands it
She is my goddess
my salvation
I must fulfill Her desires

I have dedicated my life
my art to the *Virgen de Guadalupe*
no one can ban
this sacred relationship

Nobody can take Her gift away from me
I love Her   She is unconditional love

Morena Survivor on Andalusian Sand

Moroccan dark reddish-brown curly hair green eyes
sharp nose full African gaze educated English French speaker
full red lips smiles dreams of a *morena*'s new life

Though unwanted by Spain steps off a slow barge
a quarter-mile swim her uprooted body stands firm
a survivor on Andalusian sand

She hides behind rocks she sleeps the sun rises the beach fills
with *guiris* German French Spanish families invisible nobody notices
her fear hunger her blank lost eyes she tries to walk the beach
nonchalantly like she belongs

An open bar too expensive she figures fifty euros in a plastic bag
worries thirsty she sits at a table distant alone she asks the waiter
una coca   the waiter nods smiles leaves

A sudden panic grips her where's the money she loosens her belt
reaches under her pants children play laugh and scream on the beach
in the palm of her hands the damp euros and a note with an address

The waiter brings a tall *coca* and *un trozo de tortilla*
¡Mira! he makes a gesture toward the beach boardwalk
she sees two *Guardia Civil* officers coming her direction

¡Ven conmigo! Come! she follows him to the women's
SERVICIOS "Lock door. I come twenty minutes."
The waiter returns and takes her back to her table
No volverán. They come once no return

She wonders why he helps her she sips slowly eats
little bites of the generous slice of *tortilla* she places
a five-euro note on the table he pushes to her

He offers a small glass of red wine *Toma, este tinto te calma.*
"I speak English like you. Relax." The deep red wine moistens
her mouth he wonders what it would be like to kiss her

His tall body stands by her he doesn't back away
there is an immediate comfort between them
his light complexion hand grazes hers he has brown eyes
black wavy hair his father is *mestizo mexicano* his mother
Irish Norwegian

He understands she needs help her clothes damp no shoes
she finishes the last of the wine walks away from the bar
she covers her head with a gray scarf suddenly removes it
jams it in a small cloth bag she walks

He follows feels an unexplainable attraction to her
she strolls not in any particular direction turns right
and again goes right five blocks later the girl stands obviously
confused no doubt she is lost but can't admit to that fact
fearful of the *Guardia Civil* she moves faster to a bench
in a plush green park with her hands clenched on her lap stares
angrily across the grass toward the sea

The bright intense Andalusian sun pulsates on her
she reaches for a fragile wet folded missive that she
carefully opens and flattens on the bench struggles to read
what the sea has taken away tears cover her blouse as she
sits glaring at the blank white sheet

He remembers how he felt when he crossed the border
the first time separated from his mother by the *coyote*
pushed into another truck that drove him to the other side
alone not knowing what to do he spoke with few English
words at least he had a name address telephone and city of
an uncle written on a small white dinner napkin in his wallet

She crossed an ancient sea swam a quarter mile to shore
to the city where somebody would pick her up take
her to a safe place

He knows salt water erases information
about her contact no matter how much she tries
nothing of that history is in her memory but in the Mediterranean
under a hot golden sun in the bluest sky of the southern Spanish coast

Pura cábula

Writers have multiple faces
bodies obscenity horror
savagery decency delights
gentleness deceits love
hate pain and dreams
reside, hide deep in soul
la neta es que if this
surfaced at the same time
the writer would emerge
agonizingly contorted grotesque
unrecognizable mystifying
enigmatic whole
the sacred marvelous
flailing a self-image
unbearable to behold
only interpretation in
the lens' eye
a beast in the Aleph

AFTERWORD:
A Look Back

Margarita López López, Ph.D.

At the center of the neighbor's backyard in *barrio* Simons, a giant zapote tree soars in the eyes of a young boy struck with amazement. This impression marks the inception of *Zapote Tree*, the debut collection of poems by Alejandro Morales. The poetic dimension legendary in his prose emanates, now, from his childhood memory of this colossus and in its metaphorical representations of himself, his friends and family, his community, and others in his life. His life—past, present, and future—comes to light and coalesces in various poetic interpretations embodied in the roots, trunk, and branches of his *Zapote Tree*. In essence, these verses build on Morales' distinction as a multifaceted writer, deepening his oeuvre by veering from his visionary historiographic metafiction to an intimate gaze of his world through poetry.

Morales presents a plethora of themes semantically related to each of the book's three sections. For instance, in "Roots"—symbolized by the essence of its characters—he praises the essential nurturing relations of family, friends, neighbors, and the writer himself: i.e., those in Morales' life or the life of his zapote tree. The unforeseen poet "residing/ hiding/ layered/ deep " in the first poem, "The Writer in Me," emerges reassured by the wise old man from his childhood whose advice resonates to "forge the sword/ of the brave," in "*El compadrito.*" The poet inscribes for perpetuity the nostalgia of that which no longer is: his *barrio* Simons turning into "upside-down/ gray tears" by expiring flames in "Gray Tears"; his "Zapote Tree Sweetest Memory" of his mother's "embrace/ warm and safe"; his "mother's beautiful/ profile" in "We Ate Breakfast." Moreover, in "Defend the Story," the poet with his spirited pen, a cavalier's sword, bravely champions an epic story, ". . . a massive novel / for centuries bound / . . . the narrative episodes" of ". . . human gifts," now ". . . rendered in verse." Thus, Morales gallantly adds his Nezahualcóyotl poetic talent to his literary arsenal, while defiantly reaffirming a history of human toil and existence.

Morales combines his lexical inventiveness and thematic vigor, integral in his narrative, to create an ideological fusion about life. The space-temporal dimension prevalent in *Zapote Tree* is combined with nature's mythical circularity in "Two Snakes." The character Mary is visited by two of nature's creatures: first, "a scaled bird" that ". . . slipped in/ to greet to congratulate/ the new neighbor/ on the purchase/ of house and land"; and second, a "feathered serpent" who recites a poem "as she slowly/ went to her knees." It is in ". . . the eternal/ ephemeral unknown/ spaces of her new home," where Mary, who harvests the land ritually like her ancestors did, completes with "reptwofacefacingmirrortile" a symbiotic image alluding to Mexica and Christian geneses. Morales replaces the eagle atop a cactus, devouring a snake, and an Eve tempted by the snake with forbidden fruit. In their place, his fused allegory renders a modern, self-sufficient, affluent Mary. She kneels on top of a leaf compost, with a loving, feathered serpent, her Quetzalcoatl, kissing her hard-working hands as it rises "up her neck." Hence, the poet voices a universality and atemporality of human experience, an echo of culture, language, religion, identity, family, community, land struggle, displacement, genocide, and pride.

Although Morales' discernment and heritage burrow deeply into the personal in "Roots," it is in "Trunk" where his poetic voice evolves. As part of this development, the poet personifies the zapote tree's resilience and fortitude by the indomitable woman in "A Woman in the Holy Houses of Many Spirits." In an introspective litany of verses. the contrasting crescendo of strength exhibited by the woman and of fear by the poem's narrator witnessing the woman's entrance into a church ultimately culminates in praise for the magical, powerful woman. A lesson is learned: embrace the omnipresence of beauty, power, myth, and magic in everyday toils. In "Santa Monica Promenade, " the modest writer celebrates his loyal friend, the "brilliant mind kind heart," who, along with the author's family, comprise the audience at his "less-than-spectacular" book reading. The author also introduces a taste, a preamble, of creative delight into the ethereal, in time and space, in "The House in Old Greenwich." The intrigued protagonist curiously knocks on the door, hoping to meet the house's mysterious woman, but he finds himself answering and looking out, as a Cortazarian cross-gender axolotl: the male poetic voice becomes his desired female ghost. In sum, an emotional rise and fall congeal the nurturing nature of the "Trunk" as vital in the tree's life and in Morales' continuous evolution as a writer.

Morales' critical substratum and world vision, representative of his narrative, inform his intricate themes and characters in the book's final section, "Branches." The muffled voices of the characters embody the new stems—the youth—oftentimes neglected and desolate. As if in a film, in "Self-Defense," a raped teenage girl "rests on the lawn/ body opened wide sprawled/ crucified in a growing/ pool of blood." She has been shot 24 times by 2 cops deaf to community cries that she is no threat. Urgently, although subdued, the youth in "Branches" seek refuge from today's ills afflicting their lives: rape, police shootings, self-dislike, broken homes, school pressures, racism, isolation, etc. While "Branches" provides an ephemeral space for these tragic, ill-fated, mostly young, marginalized characters, the author's creativity further deepens into the ethereal, in time and space. Such is the case, in "…A Facility Deep Under Southern New Mexico," of the scientific investigator harnessing photographs of "the ancient to present collective/ memory…" or in "Programmer," whose young protagonist on what he calls his "way to liberation," becomes lost and lives in virtual reality and computer calculations that "evolve beyond his control/… in joy/ not in the world." By juxtaposing vivid images of youth connecting the past, present, and future, with silenced or isolated voices, the author communicates the demise that affects today's generation.

Alejandro Morales' poetic conception boldly unveils the "mind imagination soul" and the "… multiple faces/ bodies lives …/ love hate pain and dreams" of the writer in him to, ultimately, assume his place as poet. His verses in this collection reflect a retrospective poetry that admits the past and future in the present, and coalesces myth and surreality, in reality, with a sardonic touch. The omnipresent colossus brings forth "a beast in the Aleph," a Borgesian kabbalah through a Moralesian lens—his own *"Pura cábula"* encircling a life in *Zapote Tree*. Alejandro Morales has forged a new sword, a spirited poetic pen that has been unsheathed.

ACKNOWLEDGEMENTS

My pursuit to master the art of writing is ongoing. Throughout the course of my life as a writer, there have been writers, editors, readers, critics, and scholars whose encouragement and advice edified me to advance to the next literary project. The publication of *Zapote Tree* is the latest result of this process.

I thank Carol Penn for her steadfast literary advice and encouragement, and for selecting the poems comprising the earliest manuscript of *Zapote Tree* for submission to the publisher.

I am thankful for the insightful observations and translation by Margarita López López, whose knowledge of Spanish and English factored into each poem. Margarita realized that the zapote tree itself operated as the heart of the collection and, accordingly, grouped poems into components of a tree. Moreover, her perceptive "Afterword" points out the importance of family and community in my work. In conjunction with the absurd, volatile, random, social, political, spiritual, and magical backgrounds where I find inspiration, she discerns my ceaseless search for new possibilities in the past, present, and future.

Additionally, I want to acknowledge Francisco A. Lomelí, who provides an elegant commentary about my previous works to enhance the reader's experience with the poems in *Zapote Tree*. He recognizes this collection of poems as an account of my life and work.

Special recognition and gratitude to Thelma T. Reyna, chief editor and publisher at Golden Foothills Press. Her superb editing enhanced the quality and meanings of the poems and made *Zapote Tree* even more relevant to current times. It is a pleasure to work with Thelma. Her understanding of how poetry works and her guidance through the publishing process made *Zapote Tree* a realization.

Last but definitely not least, I thank my beloved family for their unflagging support and devotion: my wife Rohde; our daughter Alessandra, her husband Jim, and their daughter Isabela; our son Gregory, his wife Kimberly, and their children Iliana and Alex. They are my greatest treasures in life.

ABOUT THE AUTHOR

Alejandro Morales, the son of Mexican immigrants, was born in Montebello, California and lived his childhood years in Simons, the company town of the Simons Brick Yard #3, bordering Montebello. He earned his B.A. from California State University, Los Angeles, and an M.A. and Ph.D. from Rutgers University. Morales is an Emeritus Professor in the Department of Chicano/Latino Studies at the University of California, Irvine.

Morales' literary works include: *Caras viejas y vino nuevo* (1975); *La verdad sin voz* (1979); *Reto en el paraíso* (1983); *The Brick People* (1988); *The Rag Doll Plagues* (1992); *Waiting to Happen* (2001); *Pequeña nación* (2005); *The Captain of All These Men of Death* (2008); *River of Angels* (2014); and *Little Nation & Other Stories* (2014). Morales received the prestigious "Luis Leal Award for Distinction in Chicano/Latino Literature" in 2007 from the University of California, Santa Barbara.

Morales lives in Santa Ana, California and is now working on three projects: a biographical novel, a collection of short stories, and another book of poetry. Morales is considered a pioneer in American Latino literature, being one of the first authors in the 1970s to depict harsh socioeconomic conditions of barrios and to create Chicano cultural testimonies and metanarratives. His large body of work is deemed so consequential, that a forthcoming academic volume—*A Critical Collection on Alejandro Morales: Forging an Alternative Chicano Fiction**—examines his novels and short fiction in 14 insightful critical essays.

---

* Critical collection edited by Drs. Marc Garcia-Martinez and Francisco A. Lomelí. (University of New Mexico Press).

SPACE FOR NOTES

Made in the USA
Columbia, SC
31 August 2021